GREAT BATTLES AND SIEGES

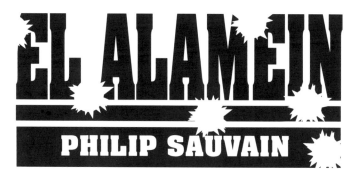

EL ALAMEIN

PHILIP SAUVAIN

ILLUSTRATIONS BY
HARRY CLOW

new
Discovery
B·O·O·K·S
New York

Maxwell Macmillan Canada
Toronto

Maxwell Macmillan International
New York • Oxford • Singapore • Sydney

GREAT BATTLES

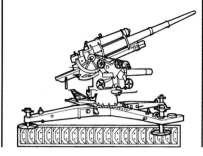

First American publication 1992 by New Discovery Books, Macmillan Publishing
Company, 866 Third Avenue, New York, NY 10022
Maxwell Macmillan Canada Inc., 1200 Eglinton Avenue East, Suite 200, Don Mills,
Ontario M3C 3N1

Macmillan Publishing Company is part of the Maxwell Communication Group of
Companies

First published in 1992
in Great Britain by
Wayland (Publishers) Ltd
61 Western Road, Hove
East Sussex BN3 1JD
England
First published in Australia by
The Macmillan Company of Australia Pty Ltd
107 Moray Street, South Melbourne
Victoria 3205, Australia

A ZOË BOOK

Devised and produced by
Zoe Books Limited
15 Worthy Lane
Winchester
Hampshire SO23 7AB
England

Printed in Belgium
Design: Pardoe Blacker
Picture research: Sarah Staples
Illustrations: Harry Clow

10 9 8 7 6 5 4 3 2 1

Library of Congress Cataloging-in-Publication Data
Sauvain, Philip Arthur.
    El Alamein/by Philip Sauvain.
    p. cm. — (Great battles and sieges)
    Includes bibliographical references and index.
    Summary: An account of the pivotal World War II battle in which the
German and Italian forces were defeated by the Allies in North Africa.
    ISBN 0-02-781081-X
    1. El Alamein, Battle of, Egypt, 1942 — Juvenile literature.
[1. El Alamein, Battle of, Egypt, 1942. 2. World War, 1939–1945 —
Campaigns — Egypt.] I. Title. II. Series.
D766.9.S33 1992
940.54'23—dc20   91-28378

Photographic acknowledgments

The publishers wish to acknowledge, with thanks, the following photographic sources:

Hulton-Deutsch Picture Library 29b; John Frost 17b, 27t; Robert Hunt Picture Library
9b, 14, 15, 17t, 26; Imperial War Museum 4, 5, 9t, 11b, 13, 18, 19, 20, 21, 25b, 29t;
Popperfoto 6, 11t, 12, 27b; Peter Newark 25t

EL ALAMEIN

Contents

At War! 4

Mussolini's Dream 6

The Afrika Korps 8

Fighting in the Desert 10

The "Desert Rats" 12

"Who Dares Wins" 14

The "Desert Fox" 16

The First Alamein 18

Monty Prepares for Battle 20

The Battle Plan 22

The Battle Begins 24

Victory! 26

Operation Torch 28

Glossary 30

Further Reading 31

Index 32

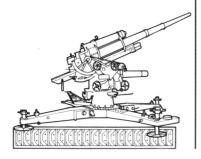

At War!

It is noon, on Sunday, September 3, 1939. William L. Shirer, an American newspaper reporter, stands in a square in the middle of Berlin enjoying the sun. Suddenly the loudspeakers in the square begin to broadcast the latest news. Britain has declared war on Germany. "When it was finished, there was not a murmur," Shirer wrote in his diary. "They just stood there as they were before. Stunned. The people cannot realize yet that Hitler, the German leader, has led them into a world war."

Later the same day, France joined Britain in declaring war on Germany. Both countries declared war because the Germans had invaded Poland. Within a few days Canada, Australia, New Zealand, and the other **Commonwealth** countries did the same. The British sent a small army to France but the Allies were too far away to help Poland in the east. The Germans waited instead for an Allied attack in the west. None came.

► *An RAF bomber flying over the pyramids near Cairo. Allied armed forces were stationed in Egypt in the Second World War to defend the Suez Canal and the Middle East oil fields.*

The First Meeting

In the late spring of 1940, Hitler's armed forces successfully invaded Holland, Belgium, and France. Major General Erwin Rommel led one of the German tank divisions, called **Panzers**. Hitler's forces cut off the British troops at Dunkirk and forced them to return to England. Major General Bernard Montgomery was one of the British commanders who was caught in that trap. Over two years later, Montgomery and Rommel met again in battle at El Alamein in Egypt in one of the most important showdowns of the war.

El Alamein

The Battle Leaders

Erwin Rommel was born near Ulm in Germany in 1891. He joined the German army in 1910 and fought in France, Romania, and Italy in the First World War. During this time he won Germany's highest award for bravery. Rommel went on to serve in the German army between the wars. When war broke out again in 1939, he was promoted to major general and given command of the 7th Panzer **Division**. This unit played an important part when the German army broke through the Allied lines in May 1940. Rommel was promoted to **field marshal** in 1942 but fell from favor in 1944. After his involvement in the bomb plot to assassinate Hitler, Rommel was given a choice: poison or trial. Thus, he was forced to commit suicide.

◄ *Field Marshal Erwin Rommel was noted for his cunning. This is why the Allied forces in the Middle East called him the "Desert Fox."*

▼ *Field Marshal Bernard Montgomery was popular with his men. He was known as the "Soldier's General."*

Bernard Montgomery was born in London in 1887. He served in the British army during the First World War and, like Rommel, he was awarded a medal for bravery. During an attack on the German trenches he was seriously wounded leading a bayonet charge. By the end of the war, Montgomery had reached the rank of lieutenant colonel. Like Rommel, he also continued to serve in the army between the wars. By 1939 he, too, had reached the rank of major general. Montgomery was commanding the 3rd Division in Belgium in 1940 when it was cut off by German tank units, one of them led by Rommel. Montgomery was promoted to field marshal in 1944, made a viscount in 1946, and died in 1976 at the age of 88.

Mussolini's Dream

▼ *Germany's Hitler (right) and Italy's Mussolini (center) were fascist dictators. They ruled by force and imprisoned and killed their opponents. Both leaders gloried in war.*

After the evacuation of British troops from Dunkirk, the German army advanced rapidly on Paris. This was the moment (June 10, 1940) when the Italian leader, Mussolini, decided to declare war on France and Britain. A New York newspaper said he did so, "with the courage of a jackal at the heels of a bolder beast of prey." Like his ally, Hitler, Mussolini was also a **fascist dictator**. Both leaders had banned all political parties other than their own. France was soon defeated and took no further direct part in the war. The United Kingdom, Canada, Australia, and other Commonwealth countries fought on.

Mussolini wanted an Italian empire as big as that of the British. He already had a North African colony in **Libya**, and now that Britain stood alone, facing the might of Germany in Europe, he seized the opportunity of enlarging his empire in Africa. The Italian army in Libya at that time was very much bigger than that of the British forces in nearby Egypt, so Mussolini ordered Marshal Graziani, the Italian commander, to capture Egypt. "That you will take it, I am certain," he said.

Graziani was a very cautious man. He was not at all certain that he could take Egypt even though he had over 350,000 soldiers at his disposal — ten times as many as the British. He knew that the Italian army in Libya was ill-equipped to fight a modern war. Its soldiers were badly led and badly trained. Graziani had many more tanks than the Allied army, but they were only light tanks with thin armor plating which was easily pierced. The Allied tanks were much stronger and heavier, and they were also armed with guns which could shoot farther than the guns fitted to the Italian tanks.

EL ALAMEIN

The Invasion of Egypt

Reluctantly, Graziani invaded Egypt in September 1940 with an army of 100,000 men. To his surprise, he met little opposition at first. Instead of pressing on, he decided to play it safe. He built a number of strong camps near **Sidi Barrani,** which was about 62 miles (100 kilometers) from the main British force near Mersa Matruh. While he took time to set up these camps, more British troops arrived by sea.

General O'Connor, the commander of the British and Commonwealth desert army in the field, was much more enterprising than Graziani. He had built up an effective tank force, the 7th Armored Division, which could move rapidly through the desert. He used it to lead a daring attack on the much bigger Italian army. Only 30,000 strong, the Allied forces advanced across the desert by night. At dawn on December 10, 1940, they took Sidi Barrani by storm. Over 30,000 Italians were taken prisoner. The rest turned and fled.

General O'Connor's tanks took another shortcut across the desert to the south, where they cut off the fleeing troops. This time they took 130,000 Italian prisoners and over 400 tanks, losing fewer than 2,000 soldiers themselves. They had won a great victory and had seized the key Libyan towns of **Tobruk** and **Benghazi.** By February 1941, they had advanced over 500 miles (800 kilometers) into Italian Libya. Had they been allowed to fight on (as O'Connor wished), the Italian forces might have been driven out of North Africa.

▼ *General O'Connor's Matilda tanks advance at night on Sidi Barrani. This victory over the Italians during the winter of 1940–1941 came as a very welcome boost to people in Britain after the bad news of Dunkirk, the fall of France, and the air raids on British cities.*

The Afrika Korps

▲ *The German Panzer Mark IV tank and 3.4-inch (88-millimeter) antitank gun. Both weapons were far superior to anything the Allies had in the Middle East at that time.*

Luckily for the Italians, help was at hand. On Wednesday, February 12, 1941, the British prime minister, Winston Churchill, issued an order. He told General Wavell, the British commander in chief in the Middle East, to send most of the Allied troops in Libya to Greece. They were to help the Greeks to defend their country. On the same day, a little-known German general called Erwin Rommel landed at **Tripoli** in western Libya. He brought with him a small German army called the **Afrika Korps** and its aim was to assist Mussolini.

Rommel's Campaign, 1941

Rommel's arrival and the running down of O'Connor's army made all the difference to the war in the desert. The Allies in Libya were now a long way from their main base in Egypt. They were badly in need of fuel. Only a small army of fresh but inexperienced troops held the Allied front line.

Rommel started his campaign on March 31, 1941, by catching the Allies off-guard. He began to push them back through Libya toward Egypt. His forces even captured General O'Connor. The Allies soon found that these German troops were a much tougher enemy to face than the Italians. They were better armed and better led.

The soldiers in Rommel's Afrika Korps were well trained. Most had fought in action before. Their Panzer Mark IV tanks had powerful 3-inch (75-millimeter) guns which could knock out an Allied tank at a range of 2,200 yards (2,000 meters), compared with the 656 yards (600 meters) needed by the Allied tanks then in service. The German 3.4-inch (88-millimeter) **antitank guns** could stop a tank at 3,280 yards (3,000 meters), three times the range of the British guns then in use.

EL ALAMEIN

Attack and Retreat

As the Germans advanced through Libya, they bypassed the port of Tobruk. Although it was held by tough Commonwealth troops, Rommel was sure that he would be able to take it later.

The Allied troops were now in full flight, but fresh troops helped them to hold the German advance at the Egyptian border. It was now Rommel's turn to be at some distance from his main supplies. His troops badly needed fuel, equipment, and men, but no reinforcements were sent. The Allies mounted Operation Battleaxe to try to rescue the troops holding out in Tobruk, but without success. Churchill, anxious for victories, replaced Wavell with General Claude Auchinleck.

On November 18, 1941 the Allied forces began a **counterattack** called **Operation Crusader**. Their soldiers had been reorganized to form the **Eighth Army** under General Auchinleck. They drove Rommel back once more into Libya and came to the aid of the soldiers still holding out in Tobruk. Operation Crusader was so successful that Rommel was pushed back almost to his starting point.

◀ *Rommel inspecting units of the Afrika Korps after they had landed in Tripoli in 1941.*

▼ *A German fighter plane landing at an airstrip in the desert. Both sides had large air forces in the desert. They played a very important part in the fighting.*

Yet again, the tide of the war in North Africa turned. Now it was the Allied forces' turn to be weakened through lack of fuel and equipment. Rommel, on the other hand, had been reinforced. He began yet another counterattack, aiming to push the Allies back through Libya into Egypt once more. For some of the Allied troops it would be their fourth trip across the Libyan desert in less than two years!

Fighting in the Desert

The weather conditions in which the two armies fought were far from ideal. It was very dry. Water was in short supply and some men died of thirst. It rained only on one or two days a year, and when it did rain, there was often flooding in the hills. Soft sandy desert turned quickly into impassable marsh and bog.

Heat, Dust, and Sand

In the desert, it was very, very hot during the day. Near the coast, however, a welcome sea breeze made the weather cooler. The great heat made it hard to see ahead clearly. People saw fuzzy images in the distance — the well-known desert mirage. The heat haze made it hard for the gunners to judge distances. Army patrols even used the mirage to escape notice as they studied the enemy lines.

▲ *A wartime magazine told its readers that the four great plagues of the desert were heat, thirst, sand, and insects.*

At night the temperature fell. Soldiers were amazed to find how chilly the desert could be at dawn when a cold wind blew toward the sea.

When vehicles moved across the desert, they threw up huge clouds of dust or sand. It was almost like fighting in thick fog. Dust and sand crept into food and drink as well as into the workings of tanks and vehicles. Keeping guns and rifles clean became a nightmare. It was worse when the wind blew across the desert, causing dust or sandstorms. In storms like these, soldiers could not see at all.

EL ALAMEIN

Tank Country

The surface of the desert, however, was often ideal for fighting in a tank or an armored vehicle. There were no rivers to block the way. There were no trees to obscure the view ahead or give cover to the enemy. Many of the desert tank battles were fought on rocky or stony ground. Where there was sand, it was often hard and gritty. These were good surfaces to travel over in a truck or tank — there were few roads. However, the hard, dry ground meant that foot soldiers had little shelter from attack. They could not dig trenches in rocky ground. They learned instead to take cover in hollows in the ground or to hide behind the low scrub which grows in the desert soil.

There were few landmarks in the desert. Each new stretch of desert was like the last. Soldiers found it hard to find their way, and a compass was essential. One Allied general was lost for two hours when he tried to find his way to the mess tent (where officers had their meals) only 1,310 feet (400 meters) away!

Both sides also had problems with the creatures who lived in the desert, such as scorpions, lizards, snails, and ants. Wherever they went, they were plagued by desert insects. They got up their noses, stuck to their lips, and crawled into the corners of their eyes. When they settled on the body, they bit hard. Many men had desert sores as a result. The only relief came at dusk when the insects disappeared with the cold night air.

▲ *Tanks advancing through the desert sand. Secrecy in the desert was difficult. Any movement on the surface threw up clouds of dust which could be seen from a great distance.*

◀ *German soldiers wearing masks during a desert sandstorm.*

11

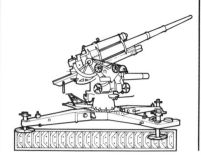

The "Desert Rats"

Rommel said that the Allied soldiers in Tobruk were caught like "rats in a trap." The name was received with delight by the men in the garrison there. They took great pride in being known as the "Rats of Tobruk." Later still, the term **Desert Rats** became the nickname of the 7th Armored Division. It is often used, however, to describe all the Allied soldiers who fought in the Libyan desert in 1940–1943.

The Allied troops were made up of a mixture of nations. There were large numbers of Australian, New Zealander, Indian, and South African troops as well as soldiers from the United Kingdom. There were also Greek and **Free French** soldiers. In 1942, the Desert Air Force was reinforced with a number of squadrons from the United States Air Force. American soldiers also served with the Eighth Army at El Alamein.

The soldiers fighting in the desert took a more casual approach to wearing uniforms than they did elsewhere. The most important thing was to keep cool in the intense heat and to keep out sand and dust. Most British soldiers wore the desert uniform of shorts and shirt called **Khaki Drill (KD)**. Australian soldiers often wore only shorts and boots. One of their officers, a major, was even seen with his badge of rank (a crown) marked in chalk on his bare suntanned shoulders.

Desert Living

The British troops lived in the tanks and trucks that carried them across the desert. There were four trucks to a platoon and thirty to a company. They kept their medical chest, food, cooking pans, water, and their own belongings on board. For much of the time the soldiers' spirits were

▶ *Although all the soldiers' food was either canned or dried, it was still possible to make an apple pie using dried apple rings. Here the pastry is being mixed in a messkit.*

EL ALAMEIN

◀ British officers enjoying a meal in the desert near Sidi Barrani in 1941.

high. They were fighting as friends against a common enemy. They even had their own words to describe their lives. The front line where the fighting took place was called "the Blue." Army biscuits were "Cruft's Specials" (after the British Cruft's Dog Show). An enemy **reconnaissance plane** was a "shufty-wallah."

There were also many hardships to endure. Most of the soldiers who lived through the war did not return home for three or four years. There

▼ Wounded soldiers at a desert hospital.

was little entertainment and daily life away from the front line was boring. They slept on the ground under the truck or in the open air, counting the stars as they went to sleep.

Water was rationed and had to be treated with chemicals, which made it safe to drink but made the milk go sour in a cup of coffee. Because it was so scarce, the soldiers used their daily ration of water over and over again for washing and for cleaning clothes.

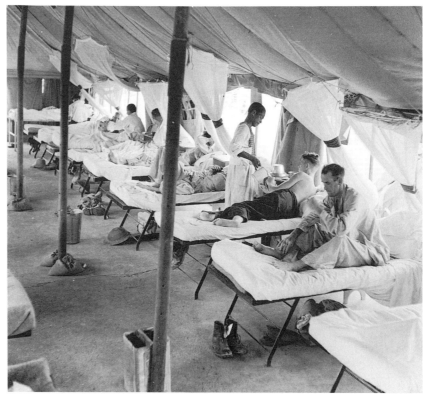

The troops lived on canned food and hard biscuits. Even the milk was canned. They lit fires with gas and used brushwood to keep them lit. Food was cooked in a small pan with folding handles, called a messkit. At night they sat around a radio to hear the news from London.

13

"Who Dares Wins"

The generals soon discovered how important it was to be able to move large numbers of troops and their supplies swiftly across the desert. Rommel even used tank carriers to bring his tanks up to the front.

Desert fighting showed up any defects in weapons and equipment. Having a gun that could fire a shell farther or more accurately than the enemy's could was vital. Time and time again a battle was won or lost because the Allies or the Germans had a better tank or a more effective antitank gun. Since there was little cover in the desert, the tank with the more powerful gun could usually hit the enemy long before he could return the fire.

Desert Fighting

Fighting in the desert was like fighting a battle at sea. In every direction the view was the same. There were endless plains of rocks, stones, and sand. This meant that there were only two things a general could do to take the enemy by surprise. He could either fight at night under cover of darkness, or he could try to deceive the enemy into thinking that an attack would come from another direction or at another time and place.

He could also send out special raiding parties to annoy his opponent. Small groups of soldiers drove through the night across the uninhabited, sandier desert to the south, behind the enemy lines. Both the Allies and

▲ *The Long Range Desert Group on patrol.*

▼ *An SAS raiding party in the desert.*

EL ALAMEIN

◄ *A German* Messerschmitt *aircraft cleverly camouflaged to make it difficult to see in the desert.*

the **Axis** forces (the Germans and Italians) had special raiding parties who fought in this way. The Germans formed a crack unit of soldiers called the *Brandenburger Afrika Kampanie.* To get past British lines they recruited about 60 men who all spoke English fluently.

The Allies, in their turn, formed the **Special Air Service Regiment (SAS)** in 1941. The regiment still fights today under the motto "*Who Dares Wins.*" In December 1941, the SAS destroyed over 90 **Luftwaffe** warplanes as they stood on airstrips in the desert. Another unit, the Long Range Desert Group, did useful work in locating the position of enemy units behind the lines. It was led by Brigadier Ralph Bagnold, a commander who had organized desert driving trips in Libya before the war, and whose knowledge of the area was invaluable.

▼ *A surprise attack by a joint British and Free French raiding party in 1942. About 200 men in 120 vehicles took part. They were led through the desert by a Long Range Desert Group patrol. Between September 11 and 20, 1942, they attacked the Italian oasis fort of Jalo, deep inside enemy lines in the Libyan desert. Although the damage they did was not serious, raids like this undermined the confidence of the German and Italian forces.*

The "Desert Fox"

Rommel was widely admired as a general during the war. His soldiers had great confidence in his ability to outwit the enemy, calling him the "Desert Fox." His tanks and guns were often fewer than those of his opponents, yet somehow he managed to snatch victory. One of Rommel's favorite tricks was to lure Allied tank units into an ambush. Then his antitank guns knocked them out as they advanced. Guns in a fixed position like this could hit a moving tank with ease. But the gunner in a tank found it hard to pinpoint a small target, such as a gun battery, while the tank was moving at any speed. The commander had to stop his tank first and then take aim.

It was exhausting and dangerous work to be a member of a tank or Panzer crew in the desert. When it came under attack, there was always the risk of being burned alive. It was also very uncomfortable. The men inside were cooped up in a small space for long periods. There was a smell of oil and unwashed bodies all the time. The tank commander, on the other hand, spent all day looking through his binoculars in the heat of the sun. Flying dust and sand blown by the wind made his eyes look like "red lozenges set in dust."

The Fall of Tobruk, June 1942

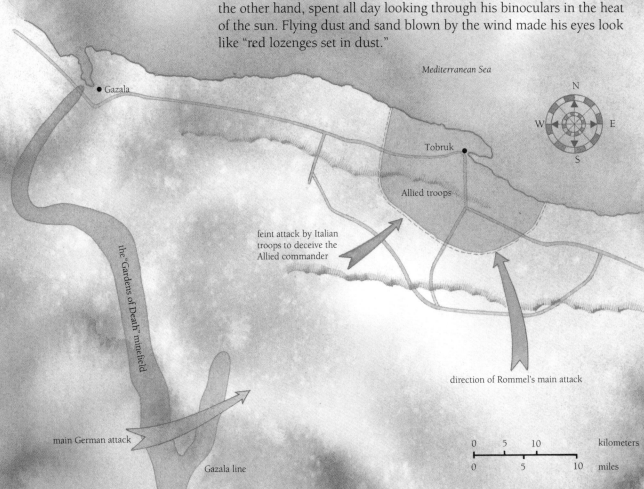

Mediterranean Sea

N
W   E
S

Gazala

Tobruk

Allied troops

feint attack by Italian troops to deceive the Allied commander

the "Gardens of Death" minefield

direction of Rommel's main attack

main German attack

Gazala line

| 0 | 5 | 10 | kilometers |
| 0 | 5 | 10 | miles |

EL ALAMEIN

Gazala and Tobruk

Following Operation Crusader in November 1941, Rommel had withdrawn and the British had relieved Tobruk. The Allied forces now needed more supplies, but none arrived. They had been sent to other war fronts instead. At the same time, Rommel received his reinforcements.

In January 1942, Rommel pushed back the Eighth Army to a position known as the Gazala line. Between the two armies lay the **minefields** called the **"Gardens of Death,"** and behind the British lay Tobruk. The defense of this important port was in the hands of a general who made the mistake of strengthening his troops in the southwest. This was the direction from which he expected Rommel to attack.

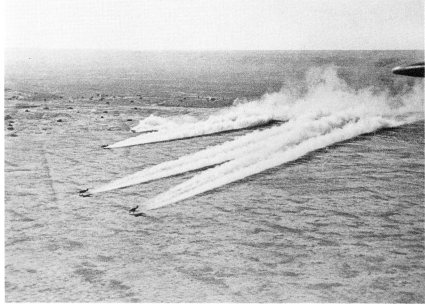

◄ *A Luftwaffe base in the Libyan desert. Both sides fought for control of the air throughout the desert war.*

▼ *Rommel on the front cover of a German wartime magazine. After the fall of Tobruk, Rommel was hailed in Germany as a great war hero.*

Rommel, the "Desert Fox," did the opposite. He sent in his Panzers from the southeast, and Tobruk fell on June 21, 1942. The Allied commander surrendered his army of 33,000 men without putting up much of a fight, which annoyed many of them. Rommel is said to have told the soldiers: "Gentlemen, you have fought like lions and been led by donkeys."

The fall of Tobruk was a great victory for the Germans. Now Rommel had access to a port which was much closer to his army in the field than had been the case before. What is more, there were huge supplies of food, fuel, and armored vehicles in Tobruk.

Tobruk was also a great **propaganda** victory for Hitler. Rommel was at the peak of his fame. He was treated as a great war hero. Hitler promoted Rommel at once to the rank of field marshal, even though he was still only 50 years of age. He was now the youngest field marshal in the German army.

The First Alamein

▶ *El Alamein became one of the best known places in Egypt during the war, yet it consisted of only a few houses and a small station on the railway line to Mersa Matruh.*

▼ *Winston Churchill (left) visited the Eighth Army himself in August 1942 to hear at first hand the plans Montgomery and Alexander had made for the coming battle.*

While Rommel and the Afrika Korps were hailed as heroes by Hitler and the German press, the Allies fell back on El Alamein, a small town (little more than a railway station) in northwestern Egypt. It was less than 62 miles (100 kilometers) from Alexandria, Egypt's main port and second biggest city. Rommel was now close to fulfilling Mussolini's dream of taking Egypt away from the British.

Rommel is Stopped

The Allies chose well when they picked El Alamein as the place to make a stand. The hard-surfaced desert which could be used by tanks was only 37 miles (60 kilometers) wide at this point. To Rommel's left was the sea, and to his right lay the **Qattara Depression**. This vast area of soft sand and marsh was impassable to vehicles. The Allies now had a much shorter front line to defend.

Under Auchinleck's command they fought this first battle of El Alamein throughout July 1942. Rommel had to acknowledge defeat. For the moment he could go no farther, and both armies seemed to have reached a stalemate. Auchinleck produced a summary of the Eighth Army's position and a plan for future action. The plan proved successful, but under another leader.

EL ALAMEIN

New Leaders, New Equipment

In spite of the first victory at El Alamein, Churchill was impatient for
further progress. When Auchinleck said that time would be needed to
retrain and supply the army, to bring about a final victory, Churchill
disagreed. He appointed General Alexander as commander in chief of
the Middle East, and General Gott as commander of the Eighth Army.
When Gott's plane was shot down and he was killed, a new man was
appointed. He was General Bernard Montgomery.

The new commander soon had more men, aircraft, and tanks than
Rommel. The United States had entered the war against Germany, with
the result that Montgomery was sent 400 American Sherman tanks and
100 antitank guns. These new American weapons were soon to be tested
in battle for the first time. They proved more than a match for the
German tanks and artillery.

Rommel's Position

The Axis forces were now a long way from their sources of supply. Fuel
was transported by road, and the carriers were often attacked by Allied
aircraft. Rommel had very real problems. However, the conditions that
made it easier for Montgomery to defend Egypt also
helped Rommel. He laid a huge mine field between
the two front lines. Half a
million antitank mines
were buried, and 15,000
smaller mines. Rommel aimed
to be ready for the next
Allied attack.

▼ The American Sherman tank, which
came into service in the autumn of
1942, was first tested in battle at El
Alamein. It proved a resounding
success. Its firepower and the thickness
of its armor plating made it a match
for Rommel's Panzer Mark IV tanks,
which up to that time had been
more effective in battle than
the Allies' tanks.

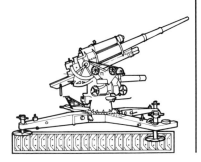

Monty Prepares for Battle

General Montgomery took over at a time when many soldiers serving in the Eighth Army were feeling very low. They had been fighting for two long years in the hot desert. Twice they had advanced hundreds of miles into Libya and twice they had been driven back by Rommel.

Montgomery immediately started to build a force which could defeat the Afrika Korps and the Italians. "Monty," as he was known to his men, was the "soldier's general." Unlike most other commanders, he could be recognized instantly. He almost always wore a sweater and a beret with two cap badges instead of one. It was his trademark. He gave his soldiers the feeling that they were on the "winning side."

Monty did not believe in taking unnecessary risks. He was always careful with the lives of his soldiers. He refused to move into battle until his army was stronger than that of the enemy. He wanted to win with the least number of casualties, which

▲ General Montgomery (left) with some of his senior officers at El Alamein. He drew up an elaborate plan of campaign after weeks of studying the land where the battle would be fought.

▶ A number of American soldiers served with the Eighth Army at the Battle of El Alamein. They were there to see how the Sherman tanks performed in battle. Montgomery's army also included soldiers from many other nations, such as France, Greece, South Africa, India, Australia, and New Zealand.

El Alamein

made him immensely popular with his men. At the same time, he insisted on instant obedience from all his soldiers and officers. Once an order had been issued, it had to be obeyed in full. He would not stand for slack or poor behavior.

Monty's caution meant that it took him two months to prepare the Eighth Army for battle. Rommel knew that an attack was bound to come, so he tried to force the Eighth Army into action before they were ready. This is why he attacked the Allied forces at **Alam Halfa** at the end of August 1942. The Eighth Army fought off the attack and Rommel had to call a halt after losing many tanks.

Meanwhile, Monty was drawing up a plan of campaign. His aim was to destroy Rommel once and for all. The Eighth Army would drive the Axis forces out of North Africa for good. He could not afford to lose, because failure would leave Egypt wide open to invasion and bring with it the loss of the Suez Canal and the oil fields.

Monty knew that American forces, led by General Dwight Eisenhower, were planning to invade northwest Africa in November. The Allies hoped to trap Rommel's forces between the two armies like a nut in a nutcracker. Montgomery was determined that the Eighth Army would play its part in this battle to its fullest. To make it clear that there would be no retreat, he sent all nonessential vehicles back to Cairo.

By the time he had finished retraining and reequipping the Eighth Army, it outnumbered Rommel's force by two to one. The Allies also had roughly twice as many tanks, guns, and aircraft as the combined forces of the Germans and Italians.

▼ *Bombs waiting to be loaded aboard an Allied bomber in the Libyan desert in 1942.*

The Battle Plan

▲ *Allied planes attacking a convoy of German and Italian trucks which were bringing vital spare parts, food, equipment, and fuel across the desert to Rommel's troops at El Alamein. Air attacks like this were as important as tank battles in destroying the ability of the Axis forces to wage war.*

Montgomery planned to break through the enemy front line in the north. It was difficult to hide his preparations, so he drew up a false plan to make Rommel think that the main attack would come from the south. This was given the code name **Operation Bertram**.

Operation Bertram

The Allied soldiers built a dummy army base in the south. The base had dummy guns and soldiers made of cardboard. Inflatable rubber tanks were put in position to deceive the enemy planes. They were moved from time to time to make it look as though a real army was preparing for battle. The Allies even began to lay a dummy pipeline. They knew that the Germans would think it could not be finished until the start of November (a week after the real battle would have started). False radio messages were also broadcast to give Germans who were listening in the impression that the attack would come from the south.

In the north, where the main attack would be launched, the Allies dug trenches near the enemy front line. They left them empty since they would be used by troops only on the actual night of the battle. The Germans, however, soon discovered that the trenches were empty. This made them suspect that they were part of a plan to make them think the attack would come from the north! To confuse the Germans even more, the Allies also put a large number of dummy vehicles in the north. Since these did not move, the Germans rightly suspected they were dummies. What they did not know, however, was that just before the actual battle, real tanks would silently take their places. This part of Monty's deception plan was highly successful. Just before the battle German headquarters sent a message to Hitler: "Enemy situation unchanged."

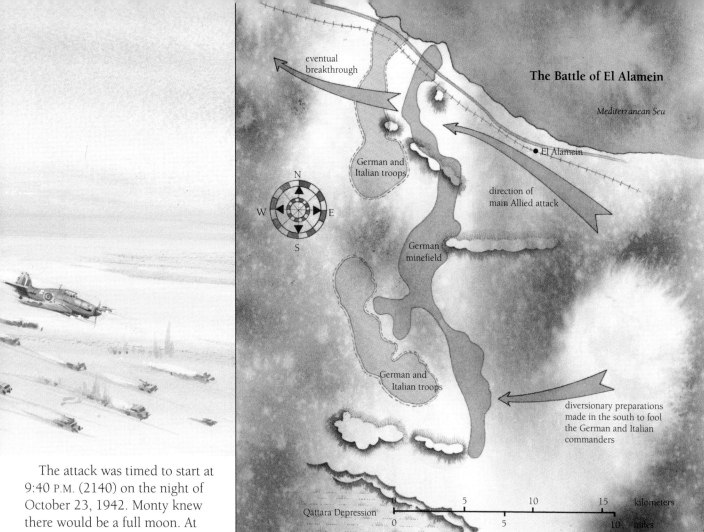

The Battle of El Alamein

Mediterranean Sea

eventual breakthrough

German and Italian troops

• El Alamein

direction of main Allied attack

German minefield

German and Italian troops

diversionary preparations made in the south to fool the German and Italian commanders

Qattara Depression

N W E S

| 0 | 5 | 10 | 15 | kilometers |

| 0 | 5 | 10 | miles |

The attack was timed to start at 9:40 P.M. (2140) on the night of October 23, 1942. Monty knew there would be a full moon. At exactly the same moment, over a thousand Allied guns would pound the German and Italian positions with shells. Under cover of this heavy gunfire, Allied engineers (called **sappers**) would clear a way through the minefields. To do this they would use special **flail tanks** and **mine detectors**. Once paths had been cleared through the minefields and marked with lamps, the Allied tanks and armored vehicles would drive two corridors through the German lines before dawn. Then Monty planned to beat Rommel at his own game. The Allied guns and tanks would be in fixed positions ready to fire with devastating effect on the German tanks as they moved into position to counterattack.

Before the battle, Monty took the army into his confidence. He told his men of the battle plan and said: "The battle which is now about to begin will be one of the decisive battles of history. It will be the turning point of the war. The sooner we win this battle, the sooner we shall all get back home to our families."

▼ *A flail tank and a sapper, the machines and the men in Montgomery's plan to deal with the mines laid by Rommel.*

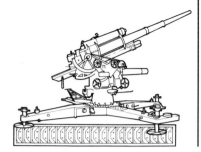

The Battle Begins

At sundown on October 23, 1942, a huge Allied army of 200,000 men waited anxiously to go into battle. It was a moonlit night — "Monty's Moon" — and a cool night wind blew inland across the desert from the sea. On all sides, the desert appeared to be in chaos as soldiers, guns, tanks, and armored vehicles tried to find their positions on the desert battlefield. A soldier who was present thought there was so much action there, it could only be a matter of minutes before the German guns opened fire and the Luftwaffe sent in to attack.

In spite of all this activity, the Germans and Italians seemed unaware of the attack to come. Two top Italian generals were on leave in Italy and Rommel himself was in Germany. He was suffering from jaundice and his doctors had sent him home in late September to recover. Montgomery knew this because the Allies had intercepted German radio messages. Rommel's replacement, General Stumme, had no previous experience in desert warfare and had had only two or three weeks to find out what was actually happening.

▼ *The gun barrage at the start of the Battle of El Alamein lit up the night sky for many miles.*

EL ALAMEIN

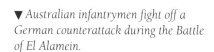

Allied Support

The Allies had one other important advantage. They had almost complete command of the air. This meant that the Axis planes were unable to provide a total picture of what the Allied forces were doing just before the battle. In addition, the German and Italian supply trucks behind the lines had been repeatedly attacked by British and American warplanes as they tried to replenish Rommel's dwindling supplies of fuel and equipment.

2140 Hours

Exactly on time, at 2140, the Allied gun barrage began. It was an awesome sight and made an even more awesome sound. Shells from over 1,000 heavy guns began to fall on the German lines at the same time. An eyewitness said there was one gun every forty feet and each gun had hundreds of shells to fire. "The guns nearby crash incessantly, one against another, searing the darkness with gashes of flame," he said. The noise was so great that it startled soldiers half a mile or more from the front line. Rommel said later that the shells hit the German gun positions "with extraordinary accuracy." The shells also destroyed the German telephone system at the front. This made it difficult for the German commanders to obtain accurate reports of what was happening.

At 2200, under cover of gunfire, groups of Allied soldiers dressed in shorts, shirts, and helmets began moving forward on foot through the minefield. Each man had a white cross on his back. It was their job to help clear the mines. As they did so, they laid white markers on the ground with hooded lanterns. They were assisted by a number of Scorpion tanks with whirling chains to set off the mines they detected. Behind them came the **infantry** with fixed bayonets to clear the way for the tanks massing behind the two corridors which were being driven through the enemy lines.

▼ *Australian infantrymen fight off a German counterattack during the Battle of El Alamein.*

◄ *Montgomery keeping an eye on the Battle of El Alamein from his personal tank.*

Victory!

▶ *Allied infantrymen force a German tank commander to surrender.*

The Battle of El Alamein lasted nearly two weeks, from October 23 to November 4, 1942. One soldier said he slept for only six hours during the first 60 hours of the battle. Throughout that time there was much fierce and bitter fighting. The German and Italian soldiers defended their positions bravely and stubbornly against overwhelming odds.

In fact, the Allied forces had several setbacks. On the first night, the gaps through the minefields were not cleared in time for the armor to get through before daylight. This caused confusion, and there was some reluctance on the part of the Allied tank commanders to press ahead. But Montgomery insisted that they stick to his plan.

Meanwhile the Axis powers sorely missed Rommel as leader. General Stumme was no substitute. The breakdown in telephone links with the front line meant that Stumme went out to see what was happening for himself. When his staff car was attacked by Allied gunfire, his quick-thinking driver immediately swung the car around to speed back to headquarters. Stumme, however, was thrown out of the car and died of a heart attack. German High Command did not know about this until 24 hours later. So, at a key moment in the crucial battle, the top German commander was missing and the Axis forces lost the chance to make an effective counterattack. In desperation, Hitler asked Rommel to return to the area at once. Rommel flew back to find chaos on the battlefield, and there was little he could do.

EL ALAMEIN

The Final Attack

On November 2, Montgomery and the Eighth Army launched the final attack, code-named **Operation Supercharge**. The next day Rommel made plans to retreat in order to save lives and keep as much equipment and as many tanks as possible. But Hitler, from the safety of Germany, ordered the German troops to stand firm. He told them their choice was "victory or death" — and then changed his mind the next day.

At last, Rommel was able to withdraw the remnants of his crack army. By that time, more than 50,000 German and Italian soldiers, including many generals, had been killed, injured, or captured. Monty's Allied army suffered heavily, too, with over 13,000 casualties, but the victory was theirs.

Rommel's defeat at El Alamein was very good news for the Allies. Bells rang out from every church in Britain to celebrate. Up to this time, most of the war news had been bad. The Germans had thrust deep into Russia and had overrun Europe. But at El Alamein, Rommel, the hero of the desert war, had suffered a major defeat. The tide of war had begun to turn. It was followed soon afterward by a great Russian victory at Stalingrad and a succession of American victories over the Japanese in the Pacific.

▼ *Victory headlines in the British newspaper,* The Daily Mirror, *on November 5, 1942.*

▼ *The massive roundup of German and Italian prisoners after the battle. These were the lucky ones. Many thousands of their comrades lay dead.*

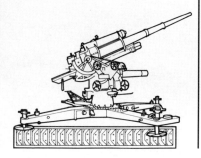

Operation Torch

Four days after El Alamein, U.S. Army General Eisenhower launched **Operation Torch**. A joint force of American and British soldiers landed on the coast of Northwest Africa on November 8, 1942. They fought their way eastward toward the Eighth Army, which was now in full pursuit of Rommel and traveling in the opposite direction. The Germans poured troops into Tunisia to stop the American advance, but, despite setbacks, the two Allied armies met up on April 7, 1943. The Italians and the Afrika Korps made a gallant last stand but it was too late. On May 12, 1943, over a quarter of a million Axis troops surrendered. The war in North Africa was over.

The Allies were now ready to invade Europe itself. On July 10, 1943, they landed on the island of Sicily and caused panic in mainland Italy. Montgomery and American General George Patton led the two Allied armies. Two months later they were in Italy and the Italian government had fallen. The German army in Italy fought on, although the fortunes of the war had now turned in favor of the Allies.

▼ *The Eighth Army parading in triumph through the streets of Tripoli during the long advance across Libya in the winter of 1942–1943. By this time they had already covered 1,054 miles (1,700 kilometers) since leaving El Alamein.*

EL ALAMEIN

◀ American soldiers landing in Normandy on June 6, 1944. Had Rommel's advice been taken, they would have faced German Panzer units on the beaches, and their task would have been even more difficult than it was.

Last Meeting

Montgomery and Rommel fought against each other for the last time in June 1944, when the Allies invaded Normandy. Supreme Allied Commander General Eisenhower put Montgomery in charge of the Allied land forces on D-Day (June 6, 1944). Monty later led one of the victorious Allied armies in an advance on Berlin. By now a field marshal, he accepted the surrender of half a million German troops at the end of the war in May 1945.

Meanwhile, Rommel had been blamed by Hitler for the Axis defeat in North Africa. Nonetheless, Hitler later put him in command (under Field Marshal von Rundstedt) of the German armies defending the coast of France. But the two field marshals could not agree on the best way to resist the expected Allied landing. Luckily for the Allies, Rommel's advice was ignored!

Even Rommel could be deceived. On June 3, 1944, he wrote in his diary that there was no sign yet of an Allied attack. On June 5 (the day before D-Day) he drove to Berlin to ask Hitler for reinforcements. The Allied invasion took place the next day. Rommel returned at once but was seriously injured six weeks later when his car was hit by a bomb from an Allied plane.

Three days after this, a bomb explosion wrecked Hitler's headquarters. A number of high-ranking German officers had plotted to kill the **Führer**. Hitler was ruthless in his search for the guilty men. He found out that Rommel had known about the plot, and on October 14, 1944, the Gestapo gave Rommel a message from Hitler: He could either commit suicide and be given a state funeral as a hero, or he could face trial and execution as a traitor. Rommel chose suicide by poisoning. He died a hero — like so many of his men before him.

▲ Hitler congratulating Rommel at the Sportpalast in Berlin in October 1942. Two years later he gave Rommel, his brilliant desert general, the choice of either committing suicide (as a hero) or dying on the gallows as a traitor.

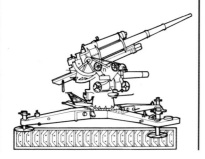

Glossary

Afrika Korps: the German desert army unit commanded by Field Marshal Rommel which fought at the Battle of El Alamein

Alam Halfa: the site of an unsuccessful attempt by Rommel, in August 1942, to lure Montgomery into battle before he was ready

antitank gun: an accurate and deadly gun designed to knock out enemy tanks before they came near enough to return the fire

Axis: the wartime alliance of Germany, Italy, and Japan

Benghazi: the main town and port of the Italian colony of Cyrenaica in northeast Libya

Commonwealth: the countries, such as Australia, India, and Canada, which were part of the British Empire

counterattack: an attack launched by an army after it has itself been attacked

"Desert Fox": Field Marshal Rommel

"Desert Rats": nickname for the Allied soldiers who fought in the desert

division: a large army unit of about 15,000 soldiers which is usually commanded by a major general

Eighth Army: the name given to the Allied desert army when it was reorganized in 1941

fascist dictator: a right-wing leader who has not been elected by the people and whose policies glorify war and military conquest

field marshal: the highest ranking officer in an army

flail tank: a specially reinforced tank that used a long whirling chain to explode mines in a minefield

Free French: a name given to the units of French Army volunteers who fought for the Allies even though France had officially agreed to take no further part in the war

Führer: the German name for leader

"Gardens of Death": the Allied name for the huge minefield which the Germans constructed in the desert as their main line of defense

infantry: soldiers who fight on foot

Khaki Drill (KD): the name given to the British desert uniform of shirts and shorts

Libya: a North African country made up of the former Italian colonies of Tripolitania and Cyrenaica

Luftwaffe: the German air force

mine detector: an instrument used to detect the presence of mines buried under the ground

minefield: an area of ground (or sea) in which mines have been concealed

Operation Bertram: the code name for Montgomery's plan to make Rommel think the Allies would attack from another direction

Operation Crusader: the code name for the military campaign which was planned to drive Rommel back across Libya in November 1941

Operation Supercharge: Montgomery's code name for the attack which finished off the German forces at El Alamein

Operation Torch: the code name for the Allied landing in North Africa four days after the end of the Battle of El Alamein

Panzer: a type of German tank

propaganda: information used to promote a cause, not necessarily the entire truth, but chosen so that the cause appears in the best possible light

Qattara Depression: the huge area of impassable, soft sand below sea-level which lies just to the south of El Alamein

reconnaissance plane: an airplane equipped with a camera which is used to take aerial photographs of the land occupied by enemy forces

sapper: an army engineer

Sidi Barrani: the site of the first Allied victory in the desert in December 1940

Special Air Service Regiment (SAS): a unit of British soldiers specially picked and trained to perform dangerous or difficult tasks

EL ALAMEIN

Tobruk: the Italian port in Libya which was captured by the British in January 1940 and held by them until it was taken by Rommel in June 1942

Tripoli: the main town and port of Tripolitania in northwest Libya

Further Reading

Harris, Sarah. *How and Why: The Second World War.* London: Batsford, 1989.

Hills, C. A. *The Second World War.* London: Batsford, 1985.

Leckie, Robert. *The Story of World War II.* New York: Random House, 1964.

Messenger, Charles. *The Second World War.* New York: Franklin Watts, 1987.

Pierre, Michael and Annette Wieviorka. *The Second World War.* Boston: Silver, 1987.

MORE ADVANCED READING

Mitcham, Samuel Jr. *Rommel's Desert War.* Chelsea, Michigan: Scarborough, 1984.

Prager, Arthur and Emily. *World War II Resistance Stories.* New York: Dell, 1980.

Strawson, John. *Alamein: Desert Victory.* London: J M Dent, 1981.

Szeming, Sze. *World War II Memoirs: Nineteen Forty-one to Nineteen Forty-five.* Boca Raton, Florida: LISZ Publishing, 1985.

Young, Desmond. *Rommel: The Desert Fox.* New York: Quill, 1987.

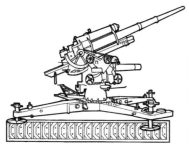

Index

Afrika Korps 8, 9, 18, 20, 28
Alam Halfa 21
Alexander, General 19
Allied army 4, 5, 6, 7, 8, 9, 12, 14, 15, 16, 17, 18, 20, 21, 22, 24, 25, 26, 27, 28, 29
    infantry 25
    sappers 23
Auchinleck, General 9, 18, 19
Australia 4, 6, 12, 20
Axis forces 15, 19, 21, 25, 26, 27, 28, 29

Bagnold, Ralph 15
Belgium 4
Benghazi 7
Berlin 4, 29
Brandenburger Afrika Kampanie 15
Britain 4, 6, 27
British army 4, 5, 6, 7, 17

Cairo 21
Canada 4, 6
Churchill, Winston 8, 9, 18, 19
Commonwealth 4, 6, 7, 9

D-Day 29
desert conditions 10, 11, 12, 13, 14, 16
Desert Rats 12
Die Wehrmacht 17
Dunkirk 4, 6

Egypt 4, 6, 7, 8, 9, 18, 19, 21
Eighth Army 9, 12, 17, 18, 19, 20, 21, 27, 28
Eisenhower, Dwight 21, 28, 29
Europe 6, 27, 28

France 4, 5, 6, 20, 29
Free French soldiers 12, 15

"Gardens of Death" 17
Gazala line 17

German army 4, 5, 6, 8, 9, 14, 15, 16, 17, 21, 22, 24, 26, 27, 28
    Panzers 4, 16, 17
Germany 4, 5, 6, 19
Gott, General 19
Graziani, Marshal 6, 7
Greece 8, 12, 20

Hitler 4, 5, 6, 17, 18, 22, 26, 27, 29
Holland 4

Italian army 6, 7, 8, 15, 20, 21, 24, 26, 27, 28
Italy 5, 28

Libya 6, 7, 8, 9, 15, 20
Long Range Desert Group 14, 15

Mersa Matruh 7
Middle East 4, 8, 19
Montgomery, Bernard (Monty) 4, 5, 19, 20, 21, 22, 23, 24, 26, 27, 28, 29
Mussolini 6, 8, 18

New Zealand 4, 12, 20
Normandy 29
North Africa 6, 7, 9, 21, 29

O'Connor, General 7, 8
Operation Battleaxe 9
Operation Bertram 22
Operation Crusader 9, 17
Operation Supercharge 27
Operation Torch 28

Paris 6
Patton, George 28
planes 4, 9, 13, 15, 17, 19, 21, 22, 25
    Desert Air Force 12
    Luftwaffe 15, 24
    United States Air Force 12
Poland 4

ports 17
    Alexandria 18
prisoners 7

Qattara Depression 18

raiding parties 14, 15
Rommel, Erwin (Desert Fox) 4, 5, 8, 9, 12, 14, 16, 17, 18, 19, 20, 21, 22, 23, 24, 25, 26, 27, 28, 29

Sidi Barrani 7
Special Air Service Regiment (SAS) 14, 15
Stumme, General 24, 26
Suez Canal 4, 21
supplies 8, 9, 17, 19, 25

tanks 4, 5, 6, 7, 8, 10, 11, 12, 14, 16, 18, 19, 21, 22, 23, 24, 25
    flail 23
    Panzer Mark IV 8, 19
    Scorpion 25
    7th Armored Division 7, 12
    7th Panzer Division 5
    Sherman 19
Tobruk 7, 9, 12, 17
trenches 5, 11, 22
Tripoli 8
Tunisia 28

uniforms 12
    Khaki Drill (KD) 12
United States army 12, 19, 21, 27, 28

Wavell, General 8, 9
weapons
    antitank guns 8, 14, 16, 19
    bayonets 5, 25
    guns 6, 8, 10, 14, 16, 21, 22, 23, 24, 25
    mines 17, 19, 23, 25
    rifles 10